CIRCUMFERENCE

by

Mark Ward

Finishing Line Press
Georgetown, Kentucky

CIRCUMFERENCE

ACKNOWLEDGMENTS

Some of these poems first appeared in the following journals:

Glitterwolf — 'Night Sweats'
Scab — 'Monsters in the Closet'
Storm Cellar — 'A School Photograph'
Tincture — 'Resisting Existence' and 'Conjugate'
Vast Sky — 'Zoetrope'

'Night Sweats' was subsequently reprinted on *The Good Men Project*.

Publisher: Leah Maines
Editor: Christen Kincaid
Cover Photography: Roscosphotography
Author Photo: William McLoughlin
Cover Design: Inkspiral Design

Printed in the USA on acid-free paper.
Order online: www.finishinglinepress.com
              also available on amazon.com

Author inquiries and mail orders:
Finishing Line Press
P. O. Box 1626
Georgetown, Kentucky 40324
U. S. A.

Table of Contents

This book is dedicated to

William McLoughlin,
Eric Thomas Norris
and Ruben Bonilla Santiago

without whom it would not exist

Circumference
Autumn 1959 / Age 35

Last week of Autumn. Sun
violent with a hollow heat.
The silence of the 1950's
ends with a chase sequence:

a tearaway with a telegram,
the weight of translated dots,
dashes, the smudged blot
blurring the broken enjamb

meant *Your father hasn't
got long* stop *Come home*
stop Is this mother
searching for similarity?

Or you, alive, engulfed by
parents still, regression
as egress renouncing
us sideways boys who

cruise like kings with
a blaze of unopened
letters that I wrote?
Or maybe you reaching

out across days lost?
Is it the boy I knew
erupting, a fed-up
firebrand unashamed?

✳✳✳✳

The intermittent man in my bed decides
tonight to talk, says *Pepperell, that can't
be a real place,* and whatever little we had
dies. I tell him to leave his key knowing

he won't and I'll have to pay to change
the locks. A diversion. They're all just
well-composed distractions, strikingly solid
and low-risk. I haven't been honest
with myself; my needs and goals don't
correlate. He silently escapes; we're not
vital enough for a door slam. Too little in
common for me to have anything to miss.

***

I don't sleep   the night
          stretches out like
days retreat   into twilight
          my missing Mike
my soul to keep   in line of sight
          a lengthy hike
haunting me   so I decide

***

An internal subsidence
has me at a bus station at dawn.
I replay their opinions word-for-word
unshifted by time or modernity
or a sense of family. I don't care that
he's dying. I wish I did.

****

I'm the only one to disembark at this
sleep-through town. It looks smaller.
My cells backsliding, I feel crushable
by a look or a well-placed noun.

My dilated eyes try to blink it all away. I wonder
if I'm too late, if that's secretly what I hoped for.

The tenderfoot son surveying the land;
its roughness, its stillness, forever
the same. I walk miles out of my way
unable to approach yesterday's ghosts.

Mother sits by the window, already dressed
in black, curtly thanks me for coming.

I balk at signs and echoes, at old neighbours
double-taking at my adult features, at schools,
at shops, at a lifetime spent wishing for a way
out from the landscape hidden under my skin;

the maps overlay the veins perfectly.
I sit with mother and she starts to speak

like years were elastic and I'd just stepped out,
like nothing happened to cause chasms between us.
For a moment, she mothers me, saying how handsome
I look before remembering the man I became.

Her lips curl with scorn, she says that I killed
my father. *Those slow deaths are the worst, the broken*

hearts, she said. Like I had wanted intimacy, she pushes
my hands away in disgust. My fingers trace the rust
of this stilled house, this late relationship, this place
to keep furniture, to watch it age, to count the days.

Night Sweats
Jan 1939 / Age 14

Everyone knows what a homo is

eyes locked to similar skin

He's not a fey boy fancying

boys who'd hate him but someone like

himself subsumed by a city

searching for some sort of signal, and then

being swallowed by it

a mind's eye consummation he's

relearning the system

nervous at visible tells

and coming out triumphant

at the end of the fairytale

monarch of his patch, barstool, apartment

and nothing else

He is a single man

almost at that age where the prefix presupposes

that society shuns

boys unwilling, unable to conform

controlled by a wilfully perverse intent

that blossoms behind eyes in sleep

that causes him to cajole boys

that don't feel like men yet

into his truck

these are just teenagers fumbling

using the gravitas he's seen

and the confidence he's coveted from

real men with

out this fear of failing the tongues

that paternal patter plied

those magic, unthinkable words

that could sate his slickness

must be known before one can speak of

his only interest, destroying innocence

he swaddles himself, trying

to still his sickness

but his fitful sleep continues to bear witness

Love
April 1939 / Age 15

It begins with letting him in
hoping that the sight of you won't
have him recoiling, muttering
something divisional, something
unoriginal and disappointing—
such a let-down possible only
with ambivalence, a not connecting
the dots between the fear of him rejecting
and the inability of naming the thing
you know better than your own breathing.

It begins with letting him win
allowing him to see what's within
without knowing if he's kin
dangling yourself out on a string—
the bait hoping to reel him in
debating if he'll see through the sting
and relate to what's behind your grin
your fixed gaze piquing his interest,
a Physique Pictorial test, a tutorial in
narrowing the space between you and him.

It begins with disappearing
sidling away from the school tour occurring
in Salem, there are side-streets to hide in,
a sense of burning impending, standing
where finger-pointing became endings.
Staring at him, he smiles, telling you to
relax. Out of your periphery you see Si
and his sycophants breaking free to smoke
nicked fags and drink their father's liquor.
You move closer, your heart free to beat quicker.

It begins with falling in, succumbing
to the blurred brawling of your lips
to the spurred calling of your lust
sprawling out across your skin
trusting the spotlight drowning out
the rest of the world, not caring who sees
this kiss, your stubble lips, this body, this bliss,
not hearing the tour guide lose it, hissing lies
that the witches deserve what they get,
these distant screams baptise our first kiss.

It begins with being oblivious, only sensing
the world when silence shocks it back in,
feeling ourselves finally slot into our skin
while our classmates have been hunting witches
and boys too big for their quickly redone britches,
the noise of which must be obvious to the mob
before us. The chorus begins to approach
as the teacher reproaches the tour guide.
There is nowhere to hide from love. In this town,
you stand your ground and stare them down.

Circumference
Autumn 1959 / Age 35

It was only after I asked
about the arrangements
and she explained them at length
that she said *He's still
alive.* Appearances however
merit decorum, require
a steady hand. *We'll drive
over in the morning.*

****

Around seven, I wake with the sun, beams
bludgeoning eyelids. My neck's full of sofa
creaks and aches.

Mother, seeing no rush to watch neon-lit death,
sleeps in. Eighteen years of familial dust layers
every surface. A life

time ago. My old room, the key waiting in its lock.
Everything untouched, cordoned off like a death
they couldn't face.

****

Years passed dissipate   The level of detail floods
            my memories, my vision
A child terrified of fate   An adult ready to spill blood
            A boy in love as abrasion
Same town, different date   nerves knead into the greater good
            The prodigal son submersion
recalls secrets one can rate   as rulebooks for where I stood

****

You, standing at the intersection, cocky,
leaning against a tree, shirt open, your hand
reaching across the armrest when the film bores
you, sloping through school, outgrowing this map,
lying in my arms listening to records deemed
inappropriate for your church's bring-and-buy,
you seeing what you saw in me, showing me too,
your teenage flaws and measured mind, the sacred
myth you sometimes wore over your informal heart,
you in every shadow of this town, a peripheral
vision trick of the light, your brightness blinding,
I look for you all over town and find you everywhere.

*****

And I miss my city, my uncrossable,
unknowable city, pockets of which I have
claimed as mine, integrated into a life
I decided. I was strong enough to return

finally. Dispel this haunting, unravel
this spell I still find in me; under eyelids,
attached to my organs, my mind, it's
an instructional parasite, the voice in the

back of your head. This place formed me.
The boy it bore died on its outskirts.
The man I became spent years only
existing. I will not engage with landscape.

****

I stop short of a visit   to your address unready
          for the answers contained
A fist of desperate digits   flex hoping to steady
          the dislodging of remains
that I won't attribute yet   to you I'm not ready
          I walk on from the refrain
with a deep breath I pivot   towards home

A School Photograph
June 1939 / Age 15

Thankfully, not alphabetically, those
strictures difficult to break,
those enforced relationships either
side of me; Maddern and Moss—
the original greeting got lost,
stuck in our throats and now
we don't speak, not even a nod,
this may seem unfriendly but it's not
the intention.
Anyway, that didn't happen.
Re-arranged by the put-upon
photographer losing the run of
thirty boys into height-based
aesthetics—there's nothing more involved
to it—we were closer than
a Stewart, M. and Martin, T.
should be but still separated
by boys without the capacity
for such a connection or sense
of time together and its commemoration. Clipped
from The Free Press, I have a picture of you
half in-frame from the parade
looking out of shot to me
hidden in my wallet. Today's setup is the
only covert way for boys to pose
together without raising suspicion.
A muttered mission, a game devised
to switch places whilst the photographer's
eyes are elsewhere elates those bored of
full uniform in sticky sun.
By the time he's ready to shoot, we're
centre-stage. I pocket-money pay for an
extra print that I persuade my mother to frame;
my civic pride thrilling her purse open.
It hangs across the room, in line with the bed so
it's the first thing I see each morning, a cover
for the other copy where I cut around us
and remove the window-dressing.

Resisting Existence
March 1940 / Age 16

night retracts revealing
the proper names of things
you sound each one out
each lipsmack drowned in
our stick-splitting footprint
flat, manageable, I rant
about our cluster of streets;
a cul-de-sac, a hamster's wheel
distant in the pale morning
boys revelling in nature,
our place in the flood
light low with approaching
dawn seeps into our bones
we own these unwalked woods
our feet in the pond, splashing
we imagine a world just for us
sunlight strengthens each moment
you stare at the torches, the
pitchforks in my eyes, the reflection
of fire in metal, in man
has me looking over my shoulder
at the slightest noise, the sunrise
leads us to the trail laid out
for us, there's only the night,
something moving in the trees,
a rustle, too scared to escape,
two foxes retreat to separate dens.

Monsters in the Closet
September 1940 / Age 16

Saturdays are spent in the dark;
a creature double feature, Mike's hand
clasped in mine, or trailing tickles
down forearms. In almost darkness
heads can find shoulders, heartbeats
slow to satiated symmetry.

Back with Boris Karloff, this week
he wears the fur of a skinned ape;
the bloody pelt slathered on him,
a roar escapes his mouth, he doesn't
recognise the pile of pale pink skin
he forgets himself and flees to freedom.

A boy-girl couple tilt-a-whirl after him
whilst we kiss through the exposition,
losing interest when the good guys close in,
preferring skin to resolution; the monster
ruined by the hero's fist, the viewer's gaze
complicit, we exit before the end, unaccredited.

Circumference
Autumn 1959 / Age 35

At lunchtime, she is ready
and suddenly impatient, irritated
by my rumpled clothes, unsuitable
for a dying father. *At least wear a tie.*
So I take one of his.

Her head darts from left to right
a tensed heron anticipating witnesses to this
harboring of me; an accomplice always
points to guilt. Confident of silence, the town is
now safe enough to slip out a stowaway.

As she drives, hands at ten and two, her meticulous
attention to the road blinkers the passenger seat, fading
past her periphery. I wonder what story she told
the town when they whispered what happened
to us that night all those years ago.

Did she marry me off to some heiress,
some lovely lonely dowager
in an unspecified state with her own estate
too far away to travel to,
too far away to visit?

Did she embellish her story of me with
misattributed photographs of a country house,
imaginary children and an unspecified but
steady, well-paid job that her friends listened to
but never once believed?

*****

Bones threaten to burst   through paper-thin skin
            but don't have the energy
They've sterilized the worst   but can't hide what's within
            I can't see an enemy

13

Only a frail man cursed   to wait for death to win
                and claim his legacy
My father, well-versed   in taking it on the chin,
                knows his body's an elegy

*****

Dad cries when he sees me, tears
trickling down see-through skin; translucent
time bridging divides. You shouldn't
see a parent cry, it erases all righteous anger

when arms as thin as flint
struggle towards your face.

I sit on the hard plastic sidecar of a chair.
His hand grasps my wrist, fingers can't close around it,
all ability to make a fist, all fight lost
with illness, the remnants of which is all he is now his

tears scratch at my chest, disappear inside my skin.
I hold his hand, he stares at our fingers

entwined. Some memory of us replays
behind flooded eyes. He tries to talk, a throat unused
to importance, he sounds like consonants
scratched and broken, struggling upwards to see light.

A glass of water, something hocked up, clear. *I can't
believe you're here.* I cry with him as he says *I'm sorry.*

*****

Beside the radiator, angled towards the window, mother
reads LIFE and TIME in silence, glancing at the clock.

Come five, she folds down the corner of her page, puts on
her coat and from the doorway, looking only at me, says

The doctor will be here soon. We can't be here
for that. It's dinnertime. There's a canteen downstairs.
Leave him to sleep. He doesn't need all this
stress. Let the doctors do their work without you hovering.

*****

The canteen is cavernous, we pick somewhere to sit
amongst the mass of empty chairs. Without meaning
to, I pray under my breath for my father, and twitch
at myself for giving in. I sound like mother.
I haven't quite forgiven him yet. I can't think past
the shock of tubes, the immediacy of the situation.
Words stumble out. *How long has he been sick?*
Her hair dangles as protector as she hunches over
her magazines. *These goddamn commies think*
they're gonna win? They're not. Never going to happen.
I ask her what she's talking about. *Do you even know*
what kind of world we're living in? And she tells me.
And shows no sign of stopping. *What happened to you?*
To him? She talks about being blown out of the sky
and how that reduces everything else, even me, even him
to nothing. *Nothing happened. This is how I've always been.*
Always able to see the world for what it is. He pretended to
be more of a man than he was. He was this soft thing full of
regret. And then she ate in sneered silence until six pm exactly.

*****

Evening drew the light out   his body bandaged in sheets
                    covered in sweat he shed
Lips crack in saline drought   the light in his eyes recedes
                    I bear witness by his bed

as he mumbles about doubt   and unsaid things he needs
           to say before he's dead
The words reach his mouth   mother's magazine ears bleed
           he bides his time instead

*****

The hospital is quiet now, a lung
hushed after a day of hard breathing.
I don't want to go. For the first time
she talks to her husband, *I'll see you*

tomorrow, okay? The *okay* insistent, definitive. She rubs his face
like she used to, a gentle caress of heart's desire, before snapping

back to what she became. She waits
at the door for me. *I don't think he's*
much time, we should stay. And her lips
chatter, spitting whispers about rules and

what would you know and *I come here every day* and *where were you*
all these years and *do you know what it's like to watch him die* and

he's asleep and I concede. *Goodbye,*
Dad. I kiss him on the forehead, no
longer surprised at forgiveness, turn
off the light and follow Mom out.

*****

The little shop is closing up for the night.
Today's news wrapped in piles, tomorrow's
fresh flowers already wilting. The last real light
on this perma-lit lobby about to go out. A shiver.

That's all. Mother trying to return her read
magazines. The vendor, a fellow Brit, is having
none of it. *It's past closing, luv. Gotta go home
and get some sleep. We're open at six.* Again,
the shiver, and I know. I run through corridors
before mother can even turn and see me leave.
I'm halfway up the stairs before she knows
I'm gone. Past nurses who've seen this before, who
know when to leave a smell alone. He's almost gone.
This is the last of us. The burden of our history, of
speeches unheard and unwritten, of years widening.
I hold his hand and cry. He's serene, fatherly. *I missed
you, son. So much. All this time and you came back
to forgive a shit like me.* I protest, *You're not—*
He coughs, *Don't contradict me. Have you any
idea how much energy this—*He falters, and I pray
to gods I don't believe in for him to finish talking,
I'm sorry for what we did. I missed you every day.
A ragged edge to every word, overdoing it, he grits
his teeth. *Letters. I kept them for you. Away from her.
My study. I'm so sorry.* His hand in mine. The machines
whirr and whine. *I love you so much.* My head on his
unmoving chest. The scream of the sound of a flatline.

Zoetrope
17th February 1942 / Age 17

A change in the quality of light,
an eyebrow twitch, my father's
backlit body haloed in the door
frame reflecting the impending—
this is what getting caught means;
being unable to move, wishing
the world away from this, terror
filling hollow limbs, shared spit
absolved by emptiness, knowing
that this is the end of the world.

Mother, half-glimpsing what is
already known in bitten finger
nails, filters us out from her
hallway hideaway. A glance is
all it takes to rewrite history.
Thoughts teem and sway like
a spun zoetrope, father flinching
at the sobering sight of us naked,
shutting out mother's grateful face,
a door slamming into its frame.

Father, too furious to find the light,
lunged at me, lit only by momentum,
moonlight; a shaft of night we moved
in and out of the room which spun
around the beam. An active turning
he was never meant to see. His fists
flurry across my body. Your scream
tries to stop it. A crack. Stomach sick.
I distract him from your escape
by making my life a series of stills.

Conjugate
17th February 1942 / Age 17

I am not what you are.
He is aware of this.
We all are.
You, a little too much, picturing what
they do together.

I was never what you are.
He cannot speak beyond the object.
We raised you—
You stare at each other, picturing what
they *do* together. What your son—

I will never be what you are.
He cannot argue with fact.
The royal we cuts off the limb.
You cauterise the wound, picturing what
they do *together*, thinking you've won.

[untitled]
19th February 1942 / Age 18

The world is the size of your parted lips. I don't notice at first that they've been split, such a reflex was the kiss. I tell you that we have to run, and you resist, and I see it; the bruises dotting your bare skin. Your broken nose, your missing teeth—the consequence of time with me. I feel my heart break inside of me and harden. *We've got to go. They'll be back any second.* I try to pull you. *We have to run.* You look at me, your spirit gone. *This is our only chance, Mike, please. Please.* All that's released are your tears washing down your bruises, spiking your fears. You flinch at the sound of a shouting voice. Your idiot cousin, the muscle, the noise, the lynchman removing all of your choice, walking toward us. You wrap yourself around me as if you could hoard us, your skin pressed against mine, trying to remember that feeling. You kiss me one last time and steeling yourself say *I'll be okay as long as you're safe. I'll find you again, I'll find a way* but it's too late. Your cousin is all fists, ready to break, to herald our fate, you off to Indiana to the doctor who will try to make you straight, me to die right here under your cousin's weight. He screams for your father and keeps punching, unbothered by the onlookers or the sound of breaking bones, only stopping for your father and the horror of our homes in his eyes. He takes over, ready to claim the prize that waits in me. He glares at you, telling himself lies that you were taken in by me. The faggot. Who deserves what he gets. Your cousin aids and abets, locking you in the car. Your father spills out invective that hurts worse than sparring until his fists run away from him. My eyes are blinded with blood. Your father, screaming of sin, is the last thing I see before they take you away from me for good.

Mike Martin, Indiana
21st February 1942 / Age 18

Don't listen to the doctors.
Don't let them alter the love
we have. They'll try to
reduce us to diagnosis.
They can never know
the depths of us. Our love
is all I've got, memories
of us as fugitives, hiding
under canopy, grasping
at being free, nights
that would never be
enough was all I got.
A knight in shining nothing,
I don't know how to win when
I'm excommunicated and you've
evaporated into thin, brittle air.
I keep rewriting this. No line
strong enough to stop a heart
drowning. No point in sending
this. No address. No. This
will reach you—don't let them
penetrate your spirit, don't listen
to their lies, just repeat them,
smile through gritted teeth and
come find me. Without you,
I don't know how to be. It can't
end like this.

Human Sacrifice
22nd February 1942 / Age 18

I dreamt that the skin of the town cracked
at its epicentre where the extinct volcano
that shaped all of New England
burst from below. Main Street gave way
to lava, a Venetian dilemma; untraversable.
Ash hovered like a plague or a snowstorm
and you were somewhere across the street.

I dreamt that my mother testified
to a hastily assembled court of men
that the devil spoke through me,
instructing her to use what wickedness
her accent provided to cause chaos
or I would destroy her family. She insists
that she did nothing and brought me here.

I dreamt that my father suggested a vacation,
driving like a man deranged, pummelling mile
markers and state lines, adhering to his own itinerary.
He seemed embarrassed of me and was unable
to speak to something so alien. He slammed on
the brakes when I asked for the restroom
and was gone before I washed my hands.

I dreamt us in an apartment, a real dump;
a twelve-storey walk-up with a broken lift
and heating on the blink. We made a world
from pictures pasted onto our walls,
a grown-up decision, each one evaluated as
surroundings. I lost myself somewhere
between your grin and the duvet.

I dreamt that I had never met you and the world
was this grey lump of nothing. I was this vacant
nightmare of a person too worn to explore
what was just below the surface, this exasperation
at the college quarterback and neighbor's son
who spent the summer shirtless but untouchable,
leading to my lonely demise in the garage.

I dreamt an end to these tales of Pepperell, a film
already in its third act, of monsters and men. The difference
between them was a shock of electricity, a short circuit
complicity becoming complication. The monsters pushed in
to the pit—the human sacrifice—cancels out the congregation's
cordial sins but you can't kill the monster, that's not how
you win. That's only how the story begins. And then I wake up.

Circumference
Autumn 1959 / Age 35

the punch, the puncture, the not-so-sure,
the out-to-lunch, the rupture, the missing cure,
the corridor, the hard light, the empty room,
the blur, the urge to fight, the moving wound,
the wall of grief, the wail, the unending,
the fraught disbelief, the frailty, the suspending,
the stories, the excuses, the sorrow,
the *sorry*s, the uselessness, the hollow

*****

A call to the funeral home puts the plan into action
like a spy given a mission. Mother disappears into
the yawning house. I sit and try to fathom darkness
through the window until my eyes sting with sleep.

*****

A silent side-street. Your mother invites me in.
My knocking fist unclenching. She says she heard
about my father. She apologises. *You don't know how much
he regrets…* The cardboard cut-out of our fight hovers over
everything. *I loved your son. You know that, don't you?*
She nods. *I haven't seen him in—I don't blame him.
My husband wouldn't—he's like your mother.* A car backfires,
she shudders. Her face clears as quick as the afternoon tea; disappeared
with a tablecloth trick. She stares at the front door. *You shouldn't—*
A readjustment. She turns away, answers the question in my face.
You of all people should understand that love isn't easy.

*****

In my head you're still   the boy bawling outside
                as the doctor discusses
the treatment of pills   and punishment applied
                as reparation for losses
that fathers want to kill   a biopsy of nerve and lies
                will cure a boy of cusses
fix his lightness of will   remove the ability to surprise

*****

The coffin is loaded and gone
by the time I get up. She is still
standing at the door, unable to
move. The house is malicious
in its silence. She grabs my hand,
willing her lips to say something
soft like *I'm glad you're here.*
She stares out into space, tests
the words in her mouth, lets them
hit her palate and the sound carry
and reverberate through her. Tears
edge around her eyes like makeup
until a hardness evaporates them.
Her hand remembers where it is
and retracts.

*****

Last walk through the world   where my father lived
                where you and I fell
in love our limbs curled   in secret it was a gift
                that I still cannot quell
the redrawn map unfurled   our places lost to thrift
                the town lost in the swell
towards home I hurled   through its lens myself I sieve

*****

Her empty house is filled with your father, screeching
insults, bad poetry. *Disrespected. Disgusting. Decency.*
My refusal to cower embarrasses. *How can you do this,*
today of all days, how could you do this? I look out,
remembering where the garden became our woods.
Your father swings and misses, falling into a cabinet.
Mother kneels, biblically. *Leave him be.* A twitch.
Why are you even here, Tommy? The mourners
creep respectfully forward. She whispers, smiling.
Show your face for an hour, then leave.

*****

I disentangle my cheek, my limbs from the fake solace,
the *I know about you* grins. *Letters.* I tear apart his

office. Nothing. *I'm missing something.* Mother.
They'd have had to be hidden away from her. The creak

that let us know he was here, pacing. I tear at the
floorboard and find a tin. Inside, a blur of my name,

faded, postmarked so long ago. About a hundred letters.
From Mike, I know. He kept them for me, his latent apology.

*****

The house is covered in empty glasses. Your father,
his fingers too close to Mother. She feels countries away.
I'm going now. I don't know what else to say.

Your father is muttering, screaming again. *I'm going.*
She whispers under him *I know.* I meet his eye.
I'll tell your son hello. He stops. *You know where he is?*

But I'm already gone. Walking without looking back,
without listening to the curtain-twitchers bitching.
My name is Tommy Martin. The one who left, leaving

again. The boy who kisses boys. The rumour.
The spectre in the flesh leaving forever. I walk
back to the bus-stop and wait, the night no longer

holding any threat. A ticket bought, I catch my breath.
A glance goodbye, I sit on the back of the bus, switch
on the overhead light and open the first letter.

Thank You

To Aimee MacLeod, Ciara Pelly, Dermod Moore, Anne Sexton, Richard Ryan, Saul Ward (no more tattoos or Karen won't let you read this!), Kiara Gannon and Emma Weafer for listening.

To the editors who first placed these poems: Matt Bright, Dominik Miles, Ben Goodney, Stuart Barnes and Punk Groves.

To the first editor who published me, Bryan Borland, who provided this book with the most beautiful blurb in the world.

To Tina McEvoy, Debra Spratt, and all the staff at the Lawrence Library in Pepperell, Massachusetts, who helped bring to life historic Pepperell for me.

To Fionn Scott for modelling, to Roscosphotography for the shot, and to Inkspiral Design for putting it all together.

To my Massachusetts buddy Ruben for showing me the lay of the land and pointing me towards the town of Pepperell, whose history and location I became fascinated with.

To my poetical brother-in-arms, Eric Thomas Norris, who read every single draft of this book, and whose insight, eye and patience made it what it is today.

To my sisters Shonagh, Richelle and Karen, and my father: words cannot describe the love and support you've given and continue to give. I love you all so much. Thank you, for everything.

To my mother, whom I miss every day, who encouraged my poetry from a young age, who brought me to the library and instilled a love of words. I would not be a writer without you.

And finally, to William McLoughlin; love of my life. Thank you for reading these poems at 2am, at 2pm, and occasionally having them read at you at some indescribable hour because I've been too excited to type them up first. You say that you don't always 'get' poetry but your words of advice always help. Waking up next to you every day means the world to me. I love you more than words can say, unless that word is lesbian.

Mark Ward is a poet from Dublin, Ireland. He was the 2015 Poet Laureate for *Glitterwolf* and his work has appeared in *Assaracus, Tincture, Poetry Ireland Review, Skylight47, The Good Men Project, HIV Here + Now, Storm Cellar, Studies in Arts and Humanities, Off the Rocks, The Wild Ones, Vast Sky, Animal, Headstuff, Emerge* and the anthologies *Out of Sequence: The Sonnets Remixed, The Myriad Carnival* and *Not Just Another Pretty Face.* He is a regular on Dublin's spoken word scene and was a featured poet in the final Lingo Festival. He founded and edits *Impossible Archetype*, a journal of LGBTQ+ poetry. This is his first book.